# BE YOUR OWN MONEY GURU

Securing Your Financial Future

Dr. Margaret Curlew

# Table of Contents

INTRODUCTION ............................................................................... 4

Chapter one ...................................................................................... 7

    Have You Secured Your Financial Future? ..................................... 7

    Secure Your Financial Future With an Internet Business ............. 9

    All of a sudden Single - Steps to Secure Your Financial Future .. 12

    Work From Home and Secure Your Financial Future ................ 16

    The Best Money Club to Secure Your Financial Future ............. 21

CHAPTER TWO ................................................................................ 24

    Money in the Well - Secure Your Financial Future ..................... 24

    3 Tips on Christian Money Management ..................................... 27

    Basic Money Management Advice ............................................... 32

    Why You Can't Improve Your Money Management Skills ......... 36

    The Benefits of Good Money Management Skills ....................... 41

Chapter three ................................................................................. 44

    Why Personal Finance Software Is Important ............................ 44

    The Best Way to Understand Personal Finance ......................... 47

    A Quick Guide to Managing Personal Finances Successfully ...... 55

    What is the Definition of Personal Finance - Budgeting ............ 58

    Cheap Personal Finance With Newly Equipped Benefits ........... 62

Chapter four .................................................................................... 67

    Debt Management Companies = Debt Free Customers ............. 67

Debt Management Plans - What Are They, and How Do They Work? .................................................................................... 74

Achieving Financial Freedom ..................................................... 78

Budget Guidelines: Four Tips for Successful Money Management .................................................................................... 82

CONCLUSION ............................................................................ 87

# INTRODUCTION

Have you secured your financial future yet? If not, what are you waiting for? Do you know how much you are worth? Are you tracking things? When was the last time you reviewed your bank statement? What were your last three transactions? Do you know? How much did you make in the last 3 months? Did all your earnings come from one source? Did they all come from the one and only source? How much have you spent so far in the last 60 days on your wants? How and when do you plan to retire?

Getting ready financially for the future can be a time loaded up with incredible nervousness. Numerous persevering individuals work for employers and rely upon their pay rates to meet monthly expenses, give investment funds, and contribute to their retirement plan. Nonetheless, investment funds, current expenses, and unexpected bills may leave the household budget-stressed. Thinking or planning about the future may not even be within your scope. We will discuss some strategies on the best ways to verify your financial future.

Making more than one stream of income is imperative. This is the mother of all financial advice. I rather say it now than wait few pages down where you won't even notice it. **Having multiple sources of income = securing your financial future.**

Depending exclusively on one paycheck can be financially limiting. If an employer chooses to slice hours or not to concede yearly pay builds, by what means will your household budget pay for necessities and meet monthly expenses? The appropriate response isn't always another occupation. Numerous people find themselves working more hours, other employment, and even thinking about a third in their constrained extra time. There are only 24 hours in a day and 7 days in a week. You can only work so much. The trick is to think, envision and execute in smarter ways than the average person.

Working for an employer can be financially limiting. The employer controls hourly wages, compensation levels, and progression openings. They frequently give little adaptability as far as booking one's time or moving past predefined pay levels. Also, salaried workers frequently work considerably more than a forty hour work week and don't even receive any compensation for their extra effort and time. Building a successful home business can prompt financial freedom and more opportunity to go through with your family, companions, and friends and family.

In the wake of working numerous years, many people find they are as yet not financially arranged for retirement. A bit of the benefit from owing your own business can be utilized to subsidize at least one retirement account, pay your children's college tuition, purchase an investment property, etc. Land and different resources that hold their value or gain income can likewise be obtained. Consider how your days of full-time retirement, semi-retirement or early retirement can be spent if your retirement accounts are adequately supported?

A home business can be worked anyplace where there is a PC with a web association. Work should be possible within the home, at a companion's house, at the cottage and on broadened get-aways. This way, work would now be able to spin around whatever side interests, exercises, and individuals you invest energy with.

# Chapter one
## Have You Secured Your Financial Future?

If you are reading this, I'm guessing your answer to the above question is NOPE. It's still not too late. As long as you are breathing, there is still hope. It's better now than never. As innovation advances, it ends up simpler for us to spend our cash on a wide range of things that don't really matter. A couple of decades prior, we just needed to stress over TV and radio advertisements; or a couple of magazines, to advance a wide range of contraptions, garments and whatever else that makes our lives helpful, or if nothing else gives us some amusement. With improved technology these days, we find ourselves spending on anything and everything like it is going out of style. Our spending habits have gotten out of control like there is no tomorrow. Oh and yes, remember to include every one of those bills that you need to pay towards the finishing of your fancy basement or outdoor pool or fancy car, etc. The inquiry is, have you verified your financial future?

This is something to consider honestly because a significant number of us are in a circumstance where we spend more than we acquire and let's be honest; life isn't getting any less expensive. Truth be told before a large portion of us know it, we are stuck in a cycle where we are working to endure, and even this isn't sufficient, so we find ourselves paying more than what we recently began with. Numerous banks and different sorts of leaders bring home the bacon out of this.

While some believe that there is nothing wrong with living a wasteful life, in all actuality along these lines of reasoning will abandon you in a troublesome circumstance as the years pass by. So by and by, have you verified your financial future? What happens when you get to a phase in your life where you can't work any longer? What happens when your children are mature enough to attend a university or college and you can't afford it? What happens if your elderly parents can no longer take care of themselves and need to be in a home? Can you afford it? All of these situations would necessitate that you have the funds to do as such. You could keep taking payday loans, salary advances, etc. However, all this will do, is just put you on the back foot, since at some point or another you will be in a circumstance where you can't take advances any longer.

Living step by step may appear to be an extraordinary "you just live once" approach, until you understand that it isn't so much the approach that isn't right, but instead how you handle that approach. By living step by step, your life will progressively wind up troublesome and tedious and will proceed on this course until the day you at last leave this world. So indeed, you live once, and with that one shot you had, you made your life amazingly hard to live in. The better approach is to have a more great arrangement in movement. As it were, you just live once, and accordingly you are going to ensure that you do things appropriately. On the grounds that everything in this life costs cash, you ought to dependably find an approach to live minus all potential limitations while in the meantime verifying your financial future. As a reward, you get the opportunity to leave this life in style!

## Secure Your Financial Future With an Internet Business

There is one thing many individuals face as they transform the curve coming into retirement that is a financial shortage. Naturally, you could maintain two sources of income and make good on higher government expenses, or you could take a gander at beginning your own online business. There are a couple of things you need to see that contrast between the disconnected world and the online world, let's investigate now.

In the alleged "Genuine World," age and experience are huge factors when work chasing. The online world couldn't care less; the money you make online isn't affected by your age.

**Online Business Ideas**

There are numerous approaches to profit online. You can move different people groups products and make a commission; this is classified "Offshoot Sales." You can construct a site and move to promote on it; this is normally known as "AdSense Sites." There are E-Commerce sites that offer products straightforwardly to clients, and you are the retailer purchasing the products discount. You can even regard sites as virtual land and get them with the expectation of flipping them. In this way, as should be obvious there are numerous approaches to make an online income, income that will secure your financial future.

**Retirement**

There are not too numerous individuals who think about the Internet as their financial life pontoon for retirement. I'll give you a couple of things to consider. You know, age isn't a factor when beginning an Internet business. Clients couldn't care less about your experience as long as the products you're moving help them. They don't give it a second thought whether you work 2 hours every day or 20, they possibly care about if your product works, and is the value point right. In some online businesses, the factors of trust and correspondence are critical; however not all.

**Love**

You know, if you cherish what you do and do what you adore, at that point life turns into a significantly more splendid adventure. Beginning your own Internet business can give you both of these things. Avoid the "brisk wealth" you will just get injured; however, don't deter your musings of owning an online business since you figure it will take to long. In a couple of years, you can have a genuinely available, financially secure online income from an unobtrusive Internet business.

There are some fundamental abilities to pick up, nothing that any sane individual couldn't do. You can't be experiencing tension to create a specific measure of income in a brief timeframe, or else the pressure will kill you. Take a gander at building an online business that will satisfy your objectives in a 1 to a multi-year period.

## All of a sudden Single - Steps to Secure Your Financial Future

Passionate factors will, in general, expect the highest rungs of your psyche, if you are confronting divorce proceedings with your spouse, isn't that right? This is flawlessly reasonable, and different issues, particularly those related to divorce and financial planning, by and large, subside to the foundation in such circumstances. By the by, Planning out your funds amid, and after, a divorce lawsuit, are of extraordinary significance, to guarantee that you have a pleasant and financially secure life, even after you end up single. These financial choices concerning divorce issues are not something that ought to be disregarded, or to be sure, deferred for thought sometime in the not too distant future either.

In all honesty, it fills no down to earth need to remain candidly ridden everlastingly, if your spouse all of a sudden chooses to abandon you. Truth be told, when you are battling a case for divorce, you would very likely need money. Thus, methodologies received in such cases should involve a regular stream of income for you, with the goal that all financial divorce-related costs can be adequately secured. The economic and the right choices that you need to take in such divorce cases are regularly somewhat entangled. Subsequently, it is perfect that you should seek special assistance from expert divorce financial planning experts in these cases.

So what precisely are the means that you need to take to guarantee that your financial wellbeing stays unblemished even in the wake of being rendered single? Divorce financial organizers, by and large, suggest specific expansive, nonexclusive rules for this reason. These recommendations incorporate reasonable economic methodologies too, and can be recorded as under:

**I) Hire An Expert Divorce Financial Advisor -** It is likely that, loaded with the intense subject matters related to a sudden divorce, you probably won't almost certainly take up the right fund choices, from the correct point of view. Henceforth, the administrations of an expert counselor ought to be employed, who might be accountable for your financial planning,

**ii) Keep The Important Documents Arranged -** When you are all of a sudden rendered single, you need to manage a few important financial reports without anyone else. These incorporate land records, wills, security declarations, a government led savings papers and bank reports, among others. Every one of these papers needs to be organized legitimately, so they can be gotten to effectively, as and when required,

**iii) Have Sessions With Your Tax Attorney -** Your organizer would continuously encourage you to contact your tax attorney, at the earliest opportunity after the divorce proceedings. That way, all your tax-related issues would stay all together,

**iv) Debt-related matters -** If you have a single existence, you are probably going to run over bills and other obligation things, collected for the sake of your now-isolated spouse, which is unpaid. You need to counsel your financial divorce expert concerning which of these bills and such liabilities you need to tidy up, and which you can send on to your spouse,

**v) Modifying Ownership Registrations -** With a divorce comes the issues of ownership of various resources that you had before held together with your spouse. An expert organizer can enable you to choose in a composed way regarding which funds and properties you ought to keep the ownership of.

**vi) Consulting A Trust Officer -** A trust officer can likewise help you in taking insightful and educated procedures, mainly when you are alone. The administration that these experts give concerning your ventures, land the executives and household financial plans are in reality precious.

It is just common that, financial issues may, in any event in the underlying stages, assume a lower priority, after a divorce continuing. Much the same as some other individual in a comparable circumstance, you are probably going to think that it is intense to ponder the passionate ramifications of being rendered single, slightly out of the blue. Reception of appropriate financial procedures is of the quintessence, to keep your financial future secure after the divorce lawsuit is finished. Contract the administrations of an expert divorce financial planning proficient, take a firm hold on the majority of your account issues and face your single life with certainty and balance.

## Work From Home and Secure Your Financial Future

Go to your most loved web news website, open a paper, watch the news on TV, and it's just about a sureness there will be included tales about the appalling condition of the economy. Joblessness is accounted for at 9%, while in truth it's nearer to 17% when you factor in the people who have quit looking. Keep in mind the days in the not so distant past when joblessness was at 5%, and many claimed financial intellectuals derided that number, saying a significant amount of those occupations were minimum wage, section level positions. In April of this current year, McDonald's reported that it was procuring 50,000 new employees, and those equivalent savants hailed it as an excellent sign that the retreat was finished. Get it's not all that awful being a passage level, minimum salaried employee all things considered.

The majority of us don't see procuring a minimum wage as an approach to purchase a home, put our children through school, pay our bills, take decent excursions, and carry on with an actual existence free of financial stresses. How would we get to that financially secure spot? Shockingly, vast numbers of us never will, since we work for other people and spend our lives exchanging hours for dollars. They get rich, and we exist, living paycheck to paycheck. We are restricted concerning what our managers choose to pay us, and never appear to excel. The future is continuously dreary.

There are a developing number of people, somewhere in the range of 30 million in the only US, who wouldn't acknowledge such a troubling financial future and took care of business. They progressed toward becoming business people - they began their very own home-based companies. Searching for business openings, they got their work done and discovered that 70% of home-based businesses will last more than three years, while just 29% of traditional new companies will make it into the third year. Can you make cash working from home? It may astound you to discover that, as indicated by the Small Business Administration, 53% of independent ventures in the US are home-based, and produce an astonishing 427 Billion in incomes every year, more than the Big Three auto organizations consolidated. Low start-up costs, low working expenses in addition to the nonattendance of employees, join in permitting people working from home to hold a lot more noteworthy offer of incomes created. The average salary of people working from home is $65,000 when contrasted with $46,000 in the general working populace. Numerous people working from home have fabricated generous six-figure salaries, and keep on acquiring those pay even in our discouraged economy.

## Loan Modification Help - Secure Your Financial Future

If you have been battling to focus on your home loan, at that point you have without a doubt been pained about foreclosure. When your regularly scheduled payments have been overdue any, at that point, you've most likely seen outrageous interest rates on your following month to month financial articulations. Also, at present, you may find yourself experiencing issues with only the negligible payment!

Loan modification can help you. If you need to work hard with your bank to change your payments, at that point, a decent loan modification legal counselor will serve you. It is profoundly vital that you can get up to speed to your debts with the goal that you won't need to concern yourself about foreclosure. Tsk-tsk, loan specialists, can be hard to deal with. Thus you may need help with your dealings.

A loan modification can make the accompanying conceivable: lower regularly scheduled payments, better interest expenses, pardoned past due regularly scheduled payments, diminished standard parity and excepting foreclosure. Regardless of whether you haven't yet been overdue on any amount if you are stolen that you may be in the close months, at that point you can, in any case, get a meet with an accomplished foreclosure legal advisor or firm.

The more you delay, the more terrible things will get. Regardless of whether you're believing that your financial circumstance will improve in the end, you need to in any case think loan modification as a choice. You shouldn't take on any bets where your home is concerned; It's always more prominent to be sheltered than frightful. If you feel that you're a prospect right now for the loan modification, or that you will be in the moving toward months, procure yourself some foreclosure help RIGHT NOW!

Approximately 2 million homeowners will be in danger of losing their homes inside the coming two years. The home loan charges and interest will proceed to rise, and a few people are relied upon to battle. You don't need to resemble these people. You need to get the foreclosure help you and your family need today to guarantee your financial future.

## The Best Money Club to Secure Your Financial Future

The best money club is comprised of people who are headed to verify their financial situating. In the past, people thought to establish work that would give a healthy retirement plan was an ultimate objective throughout everyday life. For people who would prefer not to turn their financial security over to the consideration of others, this is indeed not a satisfying game plan. Establishing and supporting your economic fate is something to be thankful for when you have the assets you need.

Having a vocation is one of the noblest conditions of situating throughout everyday life. Nonetheless, there are some who trust that a balanced out spot of business has dangers that must be considered into their financial condition. As a general rule people are thinking about approaches to protect the nature of their way of life if their business moves toward becoming tested.

Tragically, there are times when outside sources undermine businesses that have the best of aims for their workers. Those trade-offs could imply that their underlying plan to keep up a constant domain is gotten off the course of their program. This could result in pay cuts and loss of wages for workers that they esteem.

There are levels of popularity for business proprietors who need to remain in business and develop their administration or brand to an all-inclusive dimension. Promoting cost and a flighty economy weigh vigorously on their capacity to position themselves for success. This is something most business disapproved of people need to give careful thought to when they were seeking to transform their enthusiasm into a realm.

Joining yourself up with successful people who have in certainty set up for themselves a spot that you want to be is a keen choice. They have a considerable number of gifts and abilities between them can bolster you in your voyage to success. The business meeting is energizing when you are available to the process of reexamining yourself to verify a progressively settled method for living.

Being available to learning is the way to uniting any community with one shared goal. While there is a lot to get familiar with, the process is yours to encourage with the assistance of specialists that are set in positions you seek to be. The underlying and most critical errand is to be available to learning. Situating yourself for success implies you have surrendered to the process of understanding what you don't; and investigating the alternatives until you can make educated choices.

The nature of your experience will weigh vigorously upon the assets you individuals may have accessible. There is an assortment of settings that will assist you with qualifying the business sense and uprightness of your club of decision - use them. Building up your very own backup plan to approve the financial recommendations of your guides is significant to the process.

Establishing your enrollment with the best money club in your general vicinity will assist you with staying on the course of your adventure. It is essential to nourish the drive inside you that makes you feel enthusiastic about your work. Approaching an abundance of learning will enable you to sharpen your specialty and position you to be of assistance to others in your community.

# CHAPTER TWO

## Money in the Well - Secure Your Financial Future

Money resembles groundwater that floods from underneath the outside of the earth. Just the individuals who dig wells around their homes will almost certainly draw from them.

Usually for nationals in most Africa people group to reprimand the government for most, if not every open deficiency. For example, they frequently consider the specialists in charge of their absence of water supply. In the more significant part of these networks, the government is generally bumbling and questionable with regards to giving sufficient social enhancements to the whole populace, and it might be in this manner incautious to depend exclusively on them. An equal mass of that water is streaming right now in wealth underneath of your own home, yet this is my inquiry for you: do you have a well?

It may not be insightful for you to depend exclusively on the pay you procure by serving the government or any private association. Such financial supply could either be inconsistent, questionable or lacking. If you somehow managed to have your wellspring of financial salary, which is exclusively constrained by you, then you will once in a while need a supply of money.

Business endeavors resemble wells; if you can spend a significant generous total of time and money on setting them up, they could keep on creating wealth for you for whatever length of time that you live.

There is nothing as happy with, satisfying and fulfilling as having a private business undertaking that is exclusively run and overseen by you. If you can work hard to build up and manage it well, acquiring money will turn out to be very simple for you. Also, having your very own business offers you the chance to make money work for you in opposition to procuring a pay, which makes you work for money. It doesn't just give you a kind of financial freedom; it likewise ensures your financial security. Similarly, as a bottomless well can hold water in the dry spell, having your own private business will go far to promise you a consistent supply of money amid constrained income.

It isn't sufficient for you to sit tight for the rain before getting water for yourself. As opposed to sitting tight for the storm, for what reason do you not merely dig a well? The majority of the things that men dependably admire paradise for have just been given on the earth. There is a reason for the rain, and there is additionally a reason for the groundwater. It will be impulsive for you to keep searching up for the endowments of God when He has effectively given you wealth on the earth. You should merely dig your well, and when the rain falls, your well will rise, and conceivably, flood. In any case, have no well, notwithstanding when the rain falls, your favors will in any case run dry. You can appreciate the favors of God when you are working. So as opposed to hanging tight for the rain, begin working with the goal that when the rain comes, your returns will be expanded.

Similarly, you don't need to dependably hold up till the month's end before you can get money for yourself; you can generally have it at whatever point you want. The choice to wind up financially free is yours to make. Speculation openings are all over: in horticulture, in training, in data innovation, in relaxation and excitement, you are in good shape: however, if you are yet to have one, make a decision today; the ball is in your court. Choose today to wind up a business person. Be strong, be empowered, be financially free with the goal that you can have a ton of fun together.

## 3 Tips on Christian Money Management

When are you intriguing in discovering how God needs you to deal with your money? Tragically very few individuals realize how to manage their money correctly. For instance, do you ever plan to have a lot of cash by a set date; however, when the time comes regardless you're battling with your funds? The principal reason is that individuals don't have the foggiest idea of how to manage their money correctly. All together for your money management to be successful you should initially have some fundamental skills in managing your money. For those of us who are Believers, it's vital to actualize sounds Biblical practices and instructing to be effective stewards of our money.

This is the place Christian money management comes in. Proper instructive assets will encourage you to how to accurately manage your money with the goal that when you were spending plan and plan to save money, you will have it. Having proper money management will help prevent debt which will like this make a lot simpler and less unpleasant life. Simply recollect money cannot purchase satisfaction, anyway when you experience the ill effects of budgetary challenges it can bring pressure, strain, and wretchedness. God structured us to live plentifully!! He needs you to share in His wealth! Giving your accounts to God and teaching yourself properly will improve things significantly in your life. Money is the littlest piece of your funds!

Christian money management skills are critical. Teaching yourself how to properly spending plan for your necessities, will assist you with knowing when you can practically purchase your needs. You can likewise get familiar with the proper steps to contribute the money you save with money management. Although you may think you have extraordinary money management skills, there is dependably being an opportunity to get better. Here are a few hints that will assist you with getting on track and keep a decent personality. Commonly our fear is the thing that keeps us from budgetary security. The concern is a large piece of what shields us from settling on sound money-related choices.

1. **TRACK YOUR EXPENSES!!!** - It's difficult to realize how to spending plan if you don't know where your check is going. Everything from a treat for the children to new tires ought to be recorded. Be strict for a brief timeframe, and you will have a much-improved thought of where to begin your financial plan. Never wonder where your money goes again! Getting out from under terrible ways of managing cash starts with making sense of what triggers them.

2. **Have support -** Working with a companion or mentor who is taught on monetary issues, will consider you accountable and thinks about your prosperity is principal to your capacity to ace your money. No incredible competitor achieves the goal without mentors and companions cheering them to the completion. Having somebody to help you en route will give you long haul customized viewpoint for money management.

3. **Trust God! -** This sounds straightforward, yet one can't live in fear and adoration in the meantime. Concerns that are without given rein in our souls and mind start to decide our world. Realizing what the universe has in store for us and confiding in him are large pieces to settling our money-related riddle. Try not to be hesitant to profit and spend it as God expects for your life.

Christian money management is considerably more oversimplified than some may suspect. Learning the proper steps to contributing your money alongside utilizing your management skills to build your financing skills will be one of the best speculations you ever make in your future. There is a distinction in money management and being over careful. For example, utilizing your money correctly will help keep you debt free. However, being over wary can prompt misfortune openings. Extraordinary riches originates from an incredibly determined hazard.

It is safe to say that you are not kidding about money management? If you don't feel as sure as you used to look for the assistance of Christian money management mentors or advocates. They will investigate your current budgetary status while taking a gander at your management skills. If there is an opportunity to get better, they will tell you the best way to fix it. There are just positive things that can leave improving your skills. Learning proper money management can prevent bad debt, hardship and undue worry for you and your family.

When you improve your money management skills, you will before long find that when you intend to have money by a specific date whether it be for a bill or an excursion, the money will be there! This is because of the proper planning that you learn through expanding your money management skill set. A few people find that they experience severe difficulties with regards to managing money, this is because of putting your needs over your requirements. By flipping this procedure, and discovering what triggers it, you will find that you won't just save money, yet you can contribute, provide for other people and be a steward of what you have been given.

## Basic Money Management Advice

Learning how to manage money is the most vital thing that an individual can accomplish for themselves. Consider it, when you don't have a clue how to handle your money, and you will only lose all the money that you buckled down to make. What individuals don't understand is that money management is something that is LEARNED. It resembles a muscle, the more you use it, the more grounded you will be grinding away. Getting more grounded at overseeing money is fundamental to survival in this day and age. There are a lot of news tales about competitors and lottery champs that lose their whole fortune in a couple of years. For what reason is this? They don't have the foggiest idea how to MANAGE money. They are living verification that even the most extravagant individuals can lose everything they have if they don't get familiar with this critical skill.

Before looking into money management advice, it is critical to making sense of precisely WHAT it takes to manage money viable. It's extremely basic really. There are just two things an individual genuinely needs to manage money legitimately. Those things are an arrangement and self-control. That is it.

Have an arrangement. We as a whole have bills to pay. Plan your savings, plan your spending, be sorted out and track everything exchange that you make. No one else will deal with your money for you. Regardless of whether you utilize the PC or a notebook, track all your profit and spending.

Have self-restraint. It's alright to rampage spend on things once in a while, on the whole, and the principal is the bills. When your money is running somewhat tight, at that point, don't purchase that new LED TV. You genuinely needn't bother with another TV, toward the day's end you have to pay the bills and the general population charging you won't give it a second thought whether you don't have enough money to spend on time.

Since we have the very fundamental stuff off the beaten path, how about we get to some genuine money management advice! If you as of now pursue these thoughts or something near them, at that point you are as of now a decent money manager!

- Have a savings account: I put 10% of my profit aside into the bank, and never contact it. This is your savings account. It's good money to be spared and the best part about it, you gain money through premium the more money you have set aside. Try not to contact this money, and it's solitary 10% of your salary. Give it a chance to develop.

- Have an emergency fund: I spare another 10% of my money; however it's motivation is unique. This is the emergency funds. If your vehicle stalls or you can quit working, this is the money that you use to fix the issue. For what reason would it be a good idea for you to have both a savings account and emergency funds? This is because you would prefer not to burn through the entirety of your savings on an emergency. Indeed, even with an emergency you should, in any case, have set aside money. It's only a quick thought to have a reinforcement dependably.

- Organize your spending! If you discover patterns, for instance, you spend more money on cheap food than you do on staple goods, at that point you can design likewise. Discover the extravagances that you burn through money on and after that center your money onto things you need.

These are only the essentials of money management advice. If you have a reliable establishment of savings, emergency funds, and spending, at that point, you'll generally have money for everything that you use. Keep in mind, your need goes to your bills (charge card, vehicle installment, lease, and so on.), at that point everyday costs (basic supplies, garments, and so forth.), at that point saving (savings accounts and emergency funds). Only make this a propensity, and you will as of now see that you generally have an excess of money.

# Why You Can't Improve Your Money Management Skills

At first, you may believe you're improving. In any case, for correlation, how about we think about putting that equivalent time and exertion into rehearsing the piano. Would your skill level in each be similar in the wake of repeating these undertakings for a couple of hours consistently, state, over a couple of months? Possibly.

How about we stretch out that period to a year. What might you achieve on the piano presently contrasted with your money management endeavors? Shouldn't something is said about five years not far off? By this point you could without much of a stretch be performing ponders in front of an audience with that piano.

How's your money management skill and efficiency level doing? Is it true that you are as yet following that spare change on your portable application after some espresso you purchase? Now you may understand that regardless of what number of more extended periods and exertion you put into "rehearsing" money management, your skill level, and profitability will never similarly improve.

There's sole one reason your money management capability and efficiency slowed down long back yet your piano playing skills keep on taking off higher.

Allegorically and indeed, when first learning to play the piano (like learning money management), you need to initially outline where every one of the notes are on the console (where all the money is a significant part of your life), to pick up a comprehension of what's before you before you can start to play your initial two-finger tune (really begin profiting management choices). Here, is the place your money management skills get left behind, and your piano playing skills break out.

Without the slightest hesitation, when playing that piano the second time, you'd underestimate the way that every one of the notes on the console was in a similar spot they were the first time. So usually, with "work on" (doing likewise again and again a vital qualification), you're capable to recall the situation of the notes and proceed onward to the following level and work on dealing with those notes into the good skill-fabricating some portion of really playing a song.

Conversely, while dealing with your money the second time, you need to initially make sense of where every one of your notes is once more (timeframes, salary, uses, balances...) because they've all changed position since the last time you "rehearsed." It's now you may understand, the main thing you're rehearsing, is discovering notes.

If you continue dealing with your money along these lines, you'll have an entirely new console game plan (financial picture) before you every time. So basically, you're beginning once again every time. This is the reason you can't improve your money management skills to a similar degree you can develop your piano playing skills.

How about we turn this idea around, and now ask yourself, following five years, how great you would be at playing that equivalent straightforward song on that piano, if each time you sat down to play it, you needed to initially make sense of where every one of the notes was?

Possibly you perceived that issue right off the bat, so you chose to utilize the most recent innovative note-discovering programming. How's your skill level at really playing that song? Improving? What about a long time from now?

You'd come to understand that regardless of how well you aced your note-discovering capacities, your execution edge has never honestly gotten off the ground and will never get off the ground, on the grounds that your understanding, information, and knowledge of the console (your financial picture) will dependably be restricted in light of the fact that it's never the equivalent.

However at this point think about what may happen to the entire idea of money management if your money (timeframes, salary, uses, balances...) remained in precisely the same position you left them the last time...and the time before that. To get a genuine, smart thought of what that experience may resemble, merely think about the result for an artist as his skill level develops at playing that piano.

Consider for a reality that it doesn't take long for a performer to quit reasoning about the notes on the console entirely (would you be able to envision?). The performer's underlying time and exertion to "account" for the records (joke indeed proposed) usually have progressed to the association and management of the notes (song playing/money management). With time, through essential redundancy and memory, his song playing develops increasingly multifaceted and exact, while the straightforwardness and exertion at playing them turn out to be progressively rudimentary. His insight into the console has moved into an entirely instinctive state (imperceptible?), and he's currently working at a level of dominance, achieving a lot more with just the smallest of exertion.

A large number of individuals, playing out a thousand distinct exercises, are achieving dominance level ordinary. In case you're as of now putting the time in dealing with your money, there's sole one reason you can't achieve dominance level...you're confusing note-finding with money management.

# The Benefits of Good Money Management Skills

The advantages of having good money skills with regards to money management are mind-boggling. Having the capacity to manage your money effectively will open up new roads in your life that were already inaccessible because of an absence of money. Figuring out how to manage your money will give the extra cash that is required to carry on with a life unbounded. Hardly any different skills contrast with that of effective money management.

**Carry on with a More Stress-Free Life**

When you manage your money effectively, you should carry on with a more stress-free life. Money is a standout amongst the most stressful things in somebody's life and subsequently must be managed appropriately to diminish the stress required with it. Effective money management will maintain a strategic distance from a portion of the actual results that accompany not remaining fully informed regarding your bills, sending your children to school, and some other kind of stress that money conveys to one's life. If you always have some extra cash lying around you will feel substantially safer. The security that money brings has a significant impact on helping people to diminish stress.

**Accomplish Your Dreams**

Everybody has distinctive dreams in life. In any case, pretty much every thought that one can have includes money here and there or another. Having the capacity to manage money effectively is the primary way for a great many people to accomplish their dreams if they do in reality include a budgetary part. You are not going to take your accomplice on that dream vacation without money most likely. That is just not how the world functions. In any case, if you effectively manage your pay, at that point, that dream vacations turn into much increasingly sensible. Having money can enable you to accomplish a wide range of dreams other than holidays too. You may dream of sending your youngster to school or seeing your most loved pro athletics group in real to life. Whichever way risks are your dreams will cost you money and money management can be the way that motivates you to make those dreams genuinely occur.

**Travel and Take More Vacations**

While a dream vacation may not be in your arrangements, you will presumably concur that you might want almost certainly to travel more. Traveling and seeing the world is something that costs a great deal of money. For the vast majority having good money, skills are their only any desire for having the capacity to travel and see the world. There is a reason that most people with money spend it on traveling the world and seeing all that earth brings to the table with their own eyes.

**Appreciate Ultimate Freedom**

Unfortunately, in this world money influences the measure of freedom an individual has in their everyday life. When you have much money, at that point, you can do nearly anything you need. You can rest in, eat out, go to the moon, and almost anything if you have the appropriate measure of money. By accomplishing some incredible money skills with regards to money management, you can consistently open up your life to more freedom.

# Chapter three
## Why Personal Finance Software Is Important

**Why personal finance software is important**

Nowadays, innovation has truly reformed people's lifestyle, including their money-related life. Once upon a time, the vast majority utilized a pen and paper to report their profit, spending, and finances.

**What is personal finance software?**

Home finance software alludes to a money-related instrument that empowers you to set up a budget, track your costs, and check your global finances. Nowadays, there is no legitimate motivation behind why you ought to be confused and buried under water because there are numerous great personal finance programs that you can use to monitor your money, plan your future, and control your finances. If you have a PC or workstation, you are fortunate because you can undoubtedly discover great home finance software at little expense. Application software engineers have now cooked for the extreme interest for these applications as they currently accompany a wide range of capacities and abilities that can spare your money, time and exertion.

**Investigation**

You would now be able to break down your finances unaided. In any case, this sort of investigation can be a lot less demanding when you make them account foundation. Finance software will break down your significant money-related subtleties. Subtleties, for example, your month to month costs will stand out. Numerous personal finance applications additionally permit personalization. When there is one specific angle you need to think about your finances, you can necessarily make a particular examination. Numerous personal finance projects can likewise give you a month to month investigation a unique method to perceive how you spend your money on a month to month premise.

**Budget creation**

We as a whole know the significance of a personal budget. In any case, making a reasonable budget that you'll stick to is less demanding said than done. You can locate an owner finance application that creates a realistic budget for you. Enter your essential data into the software and rapidly make a straightforward budget.

**Checkbook adjusts and charges installments.**

Some of the time you'll neglect to pay charges on time. When it occurs, loan costs are more than prone to shoot up. Fortunately, you can keep up a vital separation from this misstep unequivocally. Search for a personal finance application that'll remind you when to pay your bills. In like manner, you can achieve adjusting your checkbook by merely ticking a container. Total up any sums pulled back from your record and check cautiously whatever appears to be suspicious. When you have everything on the album, it turns out to be a lot less demanding to know how your finances are faring.

**Confide in yourself and nobody else**

With regards to finances, it is ideal for monitoring all you have cautiously. You may confide in your finances with your monetary guide. However, it is as yet essential to know where each penny is at, dependable. With a personal finance application, your money will never be far from you. Regardless of whether you are paying bills, adjusting your checkbook, following your check, or making a personal budget, you ought not to live without your finance software.

# The Best Way to Understand Personal Finance

When we are attempting to understand Personal Finance, the best activity is to understand what Personal Finance isn't.

Numerous people imagine that bookkeeping and personal finance are the equivalents. However, Personal Finance isn't Accounting.

Superficially they may appear the equivalent; they both have something to do with money. Notwithstanding, the definitions will enable us to all the more likely to understand the distinctions.

Merriam-Webster's definition of bookkeeping is "the arrangement of account and outlining business and money-related exchanges and examining, checking, and detailing the results."

Given this definition, we see that bookkeeping is the way toward dissecting and recording what you have effectively done with your money.

This is the reason having a bookkeeper is generally insufficient with regards to your finances.

Bookkeepers by and large don't fret about personal finance (there are a few individual cases to this standard). Except if your bookkeeper is likewise a budgetary guide or mentor, the person will probably take a gander at what you have done with your money toward the year's end and furnish you with a report of their examination.

This report is usually your assessment form; what you owe the government or what the government owes you.

Every once in a while does the bookkeeper furnish a person with a Balance Sheet or Income Statement or a Net worth articulation; all extremely supportive apparatuses that are important to deal with your finances adequately.

Personal Finance is taking a gander at your finances from an all the more expert dynamic and objective situated point of view. This is the thing that furnishes the bookkeepers with something to record, confirm and dissect.

The Merriam-Webster's (Concise Encyclopedia) definition of "Finance" is the "procedure of raising funds or capital for any consumption. Buyers, business firms, and governments regularly don't have the funds they have to make buys or lead their activities, while savers and financial specialists have funds that could win intrigue or profits whenever put to beneficial use. Finance is the way toward diverting funds from savers to clients as credit, advances, or contributed capital through offices including COMMERCIAL BANKS, SAVINGS AND LOAN ASSOCIATIONS, and such nonbank associations as CREDIT UNIONS and venture organizations. Finance can be partitioned into three wide territories: BUSINESS FINANCE, PERSONAL FINANCE, and open finance. Every one of the three includes producing budgets and overseeing assets for the ideal outcomes".

**Individual Finance Simplified**

By understanding the meaning of "money," we can break our "own fund" down into three straightforward exercises:-

1. The way toward raising funds or capital for any use = Generating an Income.

A Business gets money through the clearance of their items and administrations. This is marked "income" or "income." A few businesses will likewise contribute a bit of their income to create more revenue (intrigue income).

A Person finds money through a line of work, or an independent company (independent work, sole ownership, organized showcasing or other private company adventure). The money coming in can be a compensation, time-based compensation, or commission, and is additionally alluded to as income.

A Government gets money through duties that we pay. This is one of the principle ways that the government creates an income that is then used to fabricate foundation like streets, spans, schools, medical clinics and so on for our urban communities.

2. Utilizing our money to profit.

The amount we spend in respect to the amount we have is the thing that makes the effect between having optimum results in our finances. Settling on great spending choices is essential to accomplishing monetary riches - paying little mind to the amount you make.

3. Getting optimum results = Keeping however much of our money as could be expected

It's not the amount you MAKE that issues - it's the amount you KEEP that truly matters with regards to your finances.

This is the piece of personal finance that everybody finds the most difficult.

Frequently people who make substantial incomes (six figures or more) additionally will, in general, spend the same amount of (or more) which implies they place themselves in the red and that obligation begins to collect intrigue. A little while later that obligation can start to develop exponentially and can crush any expectation they would have needed to accomplishing riches.

**Personal Finance made basic.**

Personal Finance shouldn't be entangled if you remember this straightforward recipe:

**INCOME - SPENDING = WHAT YOU KEEP**

For Optimal Results, you necessarily need to make more than what you spend and spend not as much as what you make so you can keep more for you and your family!

If you are not effectively progressing in the direction of an optimal result, you will as a matter, of course, get not exactly optimal results

**It indeed is that straightforward!**

Since you understand personal finance and WHAT you have to do, the following stage is figuring out HOW to do this!

The ideal approach to begin is by following these three straightforward advances:-

**1. Comprehend what you need to accomplish -** If you don't know where you are going, any street will take you there" has turned into a ubiquitous statement, likely because it is so valid. One of the propensities that Stephen Covey features in his book "7 Habits of Highly Successful People", is to begin in light of the end dependably. Knowing where you need to be will be a significant help in guaranteeing you arrive.

**2. Have an arrangement -** that you can pursue that will get you to your objectives. Knowing how you will accomplish your goals in a well-ordered method is significant. Now and then this is less demanding with the assistance of a consultant or a budgetary mentor.

**3. Use instruments and assets -** that will assist you with sticking to your arrangement and not wind up diverted by the things in life that could restrain our incomes and influence us to spend more than we should. Don't attempt and work it full scale in your mind! You will finish up with a monstrous cerebral pain, and your finances will wind up one huge dim mist!

## A Quick Guide to Managing Personal Finances Successfully

Managing your money and personal finances are simple with only a fundamental comprehension of the universe of finance. You can figure out how to deal with yourself in unpleasant minutes with this manual for personal finances, budgeting money, managing personal finances, utilizing your spending software or looking for funding help on the web. Our monetary guide offers an excellent incentive in helping you in every aspect of money.

The vast majority don't consider themselves or their lives as a business. From birth to passing, you are in store for yourself, the company of you. How you deal with your business is up to you. Similar rules that apply to maintain a successful business likewise apply to have a triumphant existence, both monetarily with your money and emotionally. Keep in mind worry around money can influence your emotions contrarily just as your wellbeing.

Giving adequate support of our kindred people is the reflection of a successful business just as offering some benefit to their lives. When you try to provide as much incentive to the same number of individuals in your life, you are sure to wind up a successful individual and clients and riches will thump at your entryway. So how does this apply to manage finances successfully you may inquire?

The following are four critical purposes of our guide from Personal Finances Online Help.com, to managing personal finances successfully.

Require additional exertion in expelling any emotion like dept uneasiness or overpower from money related commitments stress over mounting bills and income. Deporting the excitement from your finance budgeting will be a work in advancement, and you ought to dependably stay wary for over powerful feelings. Removing emotion from managing your finances will enable you to concoct special arrangements and tackle issues all the more viable.

Managing your finances all the time as opposed to letting the administrator undertakings mount up is vital. That way you remain over where you are at, can change things, settle on better decisions early as opposed to continually being in response mode or putting out flames. Keep away from decisions that would prompt liquidation like over utilizing your loans or taking on money-related responsibilities you don't have the foggiest idea of how you can pay back.

Commit yourself to create more unique ranges of abilities like budgeting, arranging and notwithstanding utilizing budgeting software. Managing personal finances like a business is tied in with seizing control of your fate, both with your finances and your life. Attempt to resemble the incredible business pioneers and assault your future with life and excitement. Regulating your funds like this, with intensity, and confidence in their significance can have astounding outcomes. Lead your money with power, and as a military, your finances are sure to pursue

Utilizing software to help you with your budgeting is a smart thought since it contains spreadsheets that have everything in one spot. You can see very rapidly where your present state is, spending better, plan better, also the time it will spare you assembling your very own spreadsheet. A definitive personal finance software gives adequate comfortable to use highlights, enabling clients to deal with each part of their finances, including accounts, investments, tentative arrangements and duties. The software will give cutting-edge data on expense laws and stock audits to support you settle on proficient decisions.

## What is the Definition of Personal Finance - Budgeting

If you end up requesting that where to start with learning appropriate finance, beginning with the definition of personal finance, budgeting, why the definition of personal finance is budgeting, we will layout in the accompanying article, because indeed there is not any more critical exercise concerning what proper monetary administration involves, and what will most specifically add to your prosperity with your money.

**Legitimate Budgeting is Personal Finance Mastery**

There is no compelling reason to look past budgeting when starting your voyage towards personal finance mastery. Budgeting can be a startling prospect when you have not done as such for quite a while, the money story told by your costs and income can paint a poor picture. Regardless of whether you are a tycoon with investments, endless loans, home loans, and stock property, or a legit dedicated individual simply starting your budgetary voyage, budgeting is the way to proceed with progress with your money.

Appropriate personal finance budgeting enables you to account for what monies you have coming in and what payments you have streamed out of your accounts. Mastery of your finances regardless of your dimension of income involves utilizing this data to settle on decisions that expansion the money you have coming in every month, and diminishing the stream of money you have left your ownership. If you accomplish this through new investments, reducing interest rates with union loans or work advancement the rudiments of personal finance budgeting continues as before.

Legitimate managing of one's obligation, income and costs is the spirit of managing your money, and that is the reason the definition of personal finance is budgeting. There is no compelling reason to get more convoluted than this, with your credit cards, payday loans, investments, and investment opportunities, you will wind up on a sound budgetary balance If you keep a nitty-gritty spending plan, pursue your money, and guarantee that you spend short of what you procure every single month.

To appropriately spending plan your finances you mainly include your wellsprings of income, account for each penny that you have streaming to you every month, and track each cost. I am not worried about the proper framework you utilize as long as you are point by point and ability your money is streaming. Track your loans, and if you have awful credit moneylenders, realize the amount you are spending in interest. Track your credit cards and what measure of your installments applies to guideline and what money goes towards interest. Make knowing your finances your business and when you have a precise image of the stream of your money, at that point work to improve your finances.

Most oversights of personal finance are made because legitimate, dedicated individuals have a dark, or foggy thought of how their money is spent from month to month. With a little consideration regarding the subtleties of your income, you will find that there are limitless approaches to spare extra money and increment your income. Maintain attention on the rudiments of personal finance and always remember that the definition of personal finance is budgeting. You also can begin making a benefit today.

# Cheap Personal Finance With Newly Equipped Benefits

From decade to decade, the modest individual fund has been giving money related help to each kind of people. It progresses amount to satisfy each little or sizable personal requests to the candidates. Cheap personal finance apportions amount that borrowers are searching for, to appear their desires in a lousy position free or straightforward way. A verified and unsecured structure characterizes cheap personal finance. If candidates have property to place for the loan, verified cheap personal finance is advertised. For people without property like occupants and non-mortgage holders, the unsecured option is structured. The unsecured option can be gotten by people who are reluctant to place guarantee against the loan.

The amount that you can obtain in cheap personal finance begins from £ 5,000 to £75,000. The reimbursement time of cheap personal finance is from 5 to 25 years. Finance reasonable secret plan permits even the terrible credit holders to get the loan and execute their interest after legal documentation. Thus, terrible loan bosses ought to outfit credit and personal subtleties decisively.

Cheap personal finance has chopped down its earlier rate of interest and offer crisp rates which each will find moderate. The interest rates shift from lender to lender in the aggressive market. Along these lines, candidates can take the benefit of this aggressive air and detect a peripheral speed which suits his reimbursement capacity.

The application technique of cheap personal finance has experienced numerous stages and has turned out to be quicker and less demanding than previously, with the adoption of the online gadget. Affirming of cheap personal finance through online technique will get the loan at the moment and furthermore it is the most very much loved application process.

The borrowers can regulate different requests in a single amount with cheap personal finance. They can buy autos, unite debts, go for occasions, redesign house, weddings, and advanced education are some favored closures which can without much of a stretch be satisfied with cheap personal finance.

## At the point when to Use Personal Finance Services and How to Find Them

Getting to be productive and prosperous will require the utilization of personal finance services and expert help to deal with your finances successfully at some phase in your life. Managing your reserve funds and Investment designs, the debt the executives, charges, and money are all piece of commercial organization that can be overpowering. There are times when utilizing services instead of managing your finances alone is a quick though.

There are circumstances when people get busy with mountain debt and finance issues that couldn't be cured throughout cost eliminating and additional positions, yet require you to utilize a service or office to enable you to oversee what you have. Such situations like separation, a tough time of joblessness, out of the blue gigantic doctor's visit expenses, contract organizations undermining to dispossess your home and so forth will require expert help to explore you out of inconvenience as well as remove some worry from your life.

These are unpleasant issues nobody gotten a kick out of the chance to engage with and paying little mind to how hard you have attempted, you have made little advancement in hoping to find a better answer for it. Before you get worried, a personal finance service can loan some assistance to you.

There are monetary help services equipped for working with your loan bosses and inspire them to lessen interest, cycle records to get them current, and incredibly get your installments diminished. The friendly staff at these important organizations is learned in every aspect of finance, and they can find better answers for your debt issues that are 99% does not take part in insolvency.

The following are records on the most proficient method to find personal finance services taking care of business.

To start with, connect with a company through an expert relief network. Every one of the organizations which have conveyed best in class results is recorded with these networks. In this way, quit sitting idle in seeking on the web. Personal finance organizations profit by the subsidence conditions. To think about debt repayment organizations, it is reasonable to visit a free debt relief network which will find the best performing organizations in your general vicinity for nothing.

Second, take a gander at the focal points and burdens of every last one of them and see which one will help you the most. So how might you guarantee yourself from the legitimate and illicit firm? The attention here is on the word lawful. When the firm which you have picked isn't recorded with a specific network, it is unlawful. This is an essential method to distinguish tricks, and it will spare a ton of money also.

Third, If none of these offices suites your preference for managing your personal finance, it might be an excellent opportunity to counsel with an expert personal finance expert. The person offers a free introductory discussion. As a customer, you have to bring applicable assets and information and recall not to shroud any debts record. The personal finance expert will audit your information and prompt you on the best way to best continue.

You may ponder what to do and where to start. If you choose to look for monetary, it is essential to do your research on the different options. What's more, apparently the web is dependably a place to begin. When in doubt of thumb search out ten organizations or sites to view, meeting or research everyone to limit to three services at that point looks for references or tributes from the three personal finance services you have picked.

# Chapter four

## Debt Management Companies = Debt Free Customers

**Your Debt Problems**

Have you ended up in debt as of late? Are your charge card payments spiraling crazy? Is remaining mindful of your home advance solicitations making it challenging to pay distinctive obligations? Expecting this is the situation, by then there is an OK plausibility that your life, when not at work, is experienced overseeing phone calls from your creditors that abandon you down, discouraged, and sad.

**You are not the only one.**

Debt has been a devastating impact in present day times. A time of unhindered spending has prompted a time of unrivaled retreat. As of late, the problems that many accepted had passed have come back intensely. Individuals with debt problems need to realize that they are not the only one. Such a unique number of people are overseeing debt today, that the individuals who are not are the minority. Try not to be embarrassed about your debt. Quiet prompts more prominent problems, and expanded debt. Address somebody about your debt today and begin your move to a debt free life.

**Debt Solutions**

The first advice that anybody experiencing debt problems ought to be given is - get help. With the ascent in debt problems as of late, there has been a going with ascending in debt solution organizations needing to assist. Many offer free advice with no dedication. Make an effort not to kick back and let the total of your obligation create to levels over your strategies. There are presently such countless out there to help you that the underlying advance to being sans commitment could be just a phone call. Obligation Management Companies offer unique arrangements, some of which are depicted underneath:

**Obligation Management Plans**

A Debt Management Plan - generally called a DMP - is the available and adaptable method for dealing with your debt. When you are in debt to more than one creditor, numerous debt management organizations will enable you to merge your debts into one reasonable regularly scheduled payment suitable to your methods.

Debt Management Plans can be the ideal solution. DMP organizations can make it, so you never again need to manage calls from your creditors. Your favorable position charges can be diminished or even hardened. Additionally, you can do this without taking out further credits or put your home in threat.

Correspondingly likewise with all obligation arrangements, regardless, there are ensnarements to a Debt Management Plan. The installments can be extended over a longer time than anticipated when you can't meet your payments, and you should keep on paying your home loan and bills. In any case, to expect a fruitful debt solution without harmful components is, tragically, implausible. Tragically, to assume a debt solution without any repercussions is unlikely. A debt management plan might be the best choice for notwithstanding the negatives that go to it.

**Individual Deliberate Agreement**

An Individual Voluntary Agreement, generally called an IVA, can free you from debt in as meager as five years. The primary method for portraying an IVA is as a formal agreement among you and your creditors in which you commonly concur a progression of decreased payments towards your total debt.

IVAs are an option in contrast to bankruptcy and accompany significantly less hurting results. For whatever period that you have an average salary and can consent to meet set payment terms over a fixed period, you might be reasonable for an IVA. Notwithstanding, IVAs are a more exceptional measure than Debt Management Plans, and the two ought not to be muddled. A Debt Management Plan might be progressively appropriate to your circumstance. You should look for advice from a trustworthy source before focusing on anything.

An IVA offers a portion of the same advantages from a Debt Management Plan. Your debts will be combined into moderate regularly scheduled payments, calls from creditors will stop, and once obligations are discounted - you can begin over again. A portion of the drawbacks is increasing, however. You should proclaim all assets and liabilities, and any over the top assets might be stopped as payment towards your debts. You may likewise lose any fortunes, legacy, or rewards that come your way. Also, the consequences of missing payments can be brutal. An inability to consent to the IVA can prompt constrained bankruptcy.

**Bankruptcy**

Furthermore, presently, we come to a standout amongst the most unnerving words in the English language today: bankruptcy. An intense concern, bankruptcy has wide-achieving results that can be profoundly harming for a long time. When you can maintain a strategic distance from it, do. Tragically, numerous individuals can keep a strategic distance from it never again. When you can't reimburse the debt in a measure of time regarded sensible by your creditors, you might be left with next to no decision.

Bankruptcy is the last alternative. Every single other option ought to be viewed as first. With bankruptcy you will locate that every one of your assets is under risk, you may lose your home, your vehicle, your business. In any case, following a year, any debts that remain will be satisfied for you. You will be debt free.

Bankruptcy is a ghastly word, but at the same time is an important one. After bankruptcy numerous things will be extraordinary, many jobs will be more regrettable, yet many will likewise be better.

**Debt Advice**

No ifs and's or buts, debt advice is your initial step on that long and misleading street to money related freedom. This section has endeavored to clear up the contrasts between specific debt solutions and give advice on the principal methods for getting to be debt free. In any case, this section does not profess to be sufficient. There is a whole other world to these solutions that can be secured here, and the best debt advice is basically to converse with somebody; to talk with somebody and to recollect not to feel embarrassed.

Debt is anything but difficult to get into, trying to escape. Debt is a crippler, it is a fearsome foe, and it is a developing scourge. In any case, there is an exit from debt. Debt management is a developing industry, and even though it couldn't exist without obligation, the industry is brimming with individuals who need to help end debt for you. Try not to endure peacefully. Try not to give debt a chance to work around you. Get help today.

Dent lands are a debt management organization offering free advice with no commitment. They provide an assortment of choices and can repackage your debts inside 24 hours. Their group has helped a vast number of individuals throughout the years and have managed a wide range of liability. They comprehend that debt can transpire at whenever and are here to help. They need you to alongside join their great rundown of fulfilled clients.

## Debt Management Plans - What Are They, and How Do They Work?

A debt management plan is an organized repayment plan set up by an assigned outsider, helping an indebted person with reimbursement of his or her obligation. The point of debt management is to help clear the mortgages at a decreased dimension over a fixed timeframe to enable the debtor to make a new beginning with their finances.

Choosing to utilize the administrations of a debt management company might be hard. It might be troublesome for people to concede they need assistance and numerous people trust that their financial life will be winding crazy before looking for help. Looking for the aid of a debt management company early can enable you to recover rapidly and help you towards a debt-free future financially.

A debt management company can enable the average consumer to assume responsibility for their debt issues rapidly. A talented individual debt assessor can diminish or take out current dimensions of debt while helping the consumer to comprehend the components that prompted the deficit and how to maintain a strategic distance from these elements in the years to come. A decent debt instructor can enable a consumer to make a practical budget plan to carry them forward later on once the existing debt has been killed. Creating a monthly budget and keeping to it likely could be the most fundamental financial choice anybody can make; however, few people set aside the opportunity to make a budget. By showing this essential aptitude, a high debt management company furnishes its customers with mastery of remaining debt free.

How does debt management work? Right off the bat, your debt advisor will offer guidance on ways that you could set aside extra cash by taking a gander at how you budget. Your debt guide will at that point help you to carry out an appraisal of your financial situation and debts by soliciting you an arrangement from questions. By making these inquiries, they get a progressively precise image of your finances. It is fundamental that you are genuinely legit when they are experiencing your finances with you to empower the debt advisor to give you the particular help you need. This data is utilized to compute the amount you can easily stand to pay every month out of your surplus pay.

When this sum has concurred with you, your creditors will at that point be drawn nearer and requested to stop all charges and arrange an alternate repayment plan with them, which will be less demanding to deal with consistently. By and large, creditors are glad to consent to the drawings, since they know as a matter of fact, that such programs are reasonable and economical.

You at that point make a single monthly installment, which is all conveyed to your creditors for your sake. It is imperative that the payment is built into your debt management plan each month. All through the length of your project, you will probably talk with an accomplished debt advisor whom you should contact when you experience any issues while the game plan is set up.

Your debt management plan will be looked into at standard interims to guarantee that regardless it meets your conditions. When your money related circumstance changes, the obligation the executive's organization have the adaptability to most likely renegotiate installments for your benefit.

With regards to decreasing and disposing of current debt, a reputable debt management firm, for example, expressdebtsolutions.co.uk can be a powerful method to pay off past commitments and take out every one of the burdens it causes. While creditors are frequently hesitant to work correctly with consumers to renegotiate the terms of their debt, they are regularly exceptionally ready to work with a real debt management company who know the language of the charge card company or the bank. Talking a similar style, they will realize how to arrange the ideal terms on the repayment of a consumer's debt. At whatever point you end up in debt over your head, odds are a debt management administration can be a significant help.

# Achieving Financial Freedom

**Meaning of Money related Freedom**

Money related opportunity is a word that has taken excellent quality in the 21st century. It is a term that depicts a lifestyle that is usually orchestrated where no one is required to work for money to cover their costs. Budgetary opportunity sustains that one can be free of the obligations of money as long as he has set an actual existence characterizing plan to deal with his funds.

This concept does not imply that one is free of debt. In any case, it fights that debt can be characterized as an expense. While debt is a logical financial thought, an individual who has obtained economic freedom is permitted to check debt as a piece of his costs as opposed to weight to his business objectives.

Being financially free is a misconception for being rich. While we realize that rich people have several million dollars in a record, their long-run overhead costs could imply that they are not as financially autonomous as they appear. In this way, this concept is a concept sensitive to your way of life and the measure of money you need to cover it. In this point of view, financial freedom isn't as difficult to achieve as initially envisioned.

**Financial Freedom is Time Freedom**

For other people, to be financially free is identical to having an extended recreation time. The concept of time is money becomes possibly the most critical factor. In all actuality, a financially autonomous individual will see that money is time. When you can build up a feeling of time freedom, at that point that implies you are a positive way to get financial autonomy.

This standard makes one's funds to a lesser degree a worry. Characterized unexpectedly, financial freedom enables somebody to require some investment in exercises without exchanging your free time for income. It depends on tradable resources that compound after some time to cover for ordinary expenses. Subsequently, riches is made which produces additional time and money. It enables people to cut their working hours with no loss of income on account of money making exercises.

**Accomplishing Financial Freedom**

This thought requires an alternate outlook. In our excellent school training, we are instructed to work for money. In this way, we set in time to work, and after that, we get our compensation. This is the acclaimed time for money swap. Financial freedom evacuates the concept of time-and-money-swap and enables a person to make money work for them.

Accomplishing this status includes another move in the way of life and general outlook. While it is anything but painful to consider having more opportunity to contribute and do business, most office workers still locate that whatever measure of time that they ought to be set in a daily schedule. A fundamental advance in accomplishing financial freedom understands that there are approaches to make better utilization of one's time.

To achieve financial freedom, significant dispositions about the concept of money should be changed. Understanding that money is just an intention to make an end is a specific something. Realizing that nobody ought to be judged relying upon the measure of wealth they possess is another. Passing judgment on this freedom as the measure of cash held nullifies the point because at last, you won't achieve this when you are not happy with the money that you have. Keep in mind that this concept is additionally an individual perception. This perception is exceedingly identified with the dimension of fulfillment that money brings.

On another side of the coin, we should likewise evacuate the negative perception of money. While the colloquialism that "money is the base of all insidious" appears to be pertinent, believing this is dependably the situation will give an anti-agents see about making riches. Continuously put into the heart that financial freedom is a substantial undertaking up to one feels it is morally stable to make money. At last, having the correct demeanor about money will go far in managing diverse perceptions of this concept. Financial freedom is at a new perspective.

## Budget Guidelines: Four Tips for Successful Money Management

I frequently prompt people looking for MasterCard debt alleviation regardless of investigating their spending propensities before they make an assurance about the arrangement they ought to pick. Every so frequently getting relief from alarming debt is as essential as finding shrouded money you as of now have by making a workable family budget that is as yet sufficiently flexible to react to unexpected conditions that will emerge. Notice, I said WILL and not MAY develop because given the uncertainty of life, unmistakably stuff happens that lives entirely outside of our control. The accompanying dialog of budget guidelines is proposed to acquaint you with creating and dealing with the budgeting procedure effectively.

While showing up inconvenience free, budgeting can be frantically precarious. All you need do is take away what you are spending from what your income is, and that is the money you have left over for optional use. Just define some spending objectives and stay with them. Appears to be simple isn't that right? Lamentably, this isn't the situation for a great many people.

For most people, their budgets languish rout over similar focal reasons; the tips beneath will set up your budget and keep it on course.

**Tip 1 - Look at what you are spending**

Since we as a whole have special needs and wants, utilizing a foreordained budget recipe is commonly ineffective. For instance, if you drive to work each day, at that point fuel is a need thing on your plan though if you take the transport to work, you will incorporate the cost of the passage in your estimations.

The correct way to deal with making your budget is to accumulate information on what you are directly spending initially and afterward investigate that information to organize and ace that spending later on. Your examination incorporates the recognizable proof of waste and finding more affordable options in contrast to your required expenses. For instance, if you drive to work and your gas costs you $50 every week, maybe you can change to open transportation at the price of $10 per week, in this manner sparing $40 every week. You should maintain a strategic distance from any rate decides that some supposed budget specialists advocate; attainable budgeting expects you to reduce and correct your present spending until you can never again discover cuts or adjustments.

**Tip 2 - Be Accurate with the Data you list**

When you are making a rundown of your income and uses, it is crucial that you precisely record expenses and income as they are not what you conger up. Abstain from adjusting costs to the closest dollar, instead, record your payments to the last cent.

For out of pocket expenses, track them for at least 21 days. For your necessary expenses like nourishment and utilities, follow for 3 to 4 months to guarantee that you have a reasonable handle on your present costs. So remember to incorporate the latte you have each morning as you go into work, or your consumption figures won't give you a precise number of where all your money is being spent.

**Tip 3 - Do not overlook those quarterly, semi-yearly or yearly expenses**

There are a couple of things which could make your budget come up short, and disregarding those quarterly, semi-yearly or yearly expenses that you have is one that can make this occur. Make sure to incorporate things like dress, school educational cost, protection premiums, and charges. You ought to likewise include a slush reserve to deal with unanticipated expenses like vehicle fix, home upkeep, and other potential amazements throughout any year. In this way, take a gander at setting aside a little every month, and after that, your budget won't be destroyed when these consumptions are expected.

**Tip 4 - Review your Budget Constantly**

Numerous people make a budget plan and after that essentially document it, yet this is one financial instrument that must be explored much of the time. Particularly amid the initial a half year, your budget needs consistent checking and update to make it reachable. Keep in mind, your budget isn't an unchangeable reality, and is always requiring an amendment to mirror your financial reality. By watching out for your budget, you make beyond any doubt that it keeps on working for you.

The uplifting news is this, budgeting and budget follow-up is the ideal approach to wind up debt free and financially steady. Make no misstep; budgeting is diligent work; however, it yields a reap that is unmatched by some other device in your financial tool stash. Allow yourself three months, and work extremely hard at it, and you will before long start to see the adjustments in your economic circumstance. At that point, you need to keep it up.

# CONCLUSION

Regardless of whether you are an internet marketing guru or a work at home tenderfoot, there might be a free marketing stage that you have disregarded. Twitter, as such a significant number of other online networking locales, is a virtual goldmine of potential clients and endorsers. By taking advantage of the Twitter fever, you remain to gain some generally challenging to achieve shoppers.

Twitter is a site that enables its enrolled clients to post little status updates for their followers to read. This is valid superficially. Where it counts, it is an exceptionally associated and streamlined way of correspondence. The excellence of Twitter is in its effortlessness. The status updates are easy to read, easy to compose, and can be seen by a large number of individuals.

Twitter isn't the best spot to glaringly drop sales pitches each other moment. Like any sales, there is a correct way and an incorrect way to approach Twitter marketing. Most importantly, your rundown of followers ought to be your best need. Some time and care must be taken to gain some critical followers and to guarantee that they regard your sentiments and updates.

When you begin dropping sales lines on your followers, they will unfollow you right away. As I stated, there is a legitimate way for this type of marketing. The best activity is to participate in some significant discussions and endeavor to become acquainted with your followers. Talk about your industry (that is, the thing that you will attempt move), and fabricate an enthusiasm for it. Most importantly, keep up some discretion. It might entice begin directly out with some computerized tweets with your member joins included, yet this will murder your notoriety.

We realize the hardships associated with beginning another business. Partner marketing is the same. In spite of prevalent thinking, there are no easy money scams that work. Life is full of failures and opportunities. We all should set goals, and I mean high goals and expectations. We should be dedicated to reaching those goals.

Educate yourself on personal finances, money management, debt management and wealth building. Grab the bull by its horns. Take control of your life. Take control of your finances. Make it your prerogative. Be smart. Get a second job. Save the extra cash and invest it later. Grow your wealth. Start your own small business. Reinvest the profit and grow. Create more than one source of income and manage your money wisely. Secure your financial future. Be your own money guru!!

www.ingramcontent.com/pod-product-compliance
Lightning Source LLC
Chambersburg PA
CBHW020602220526
45463CB00006B/2415